Chinese Cities

Shenzhen Impressions

中国城市

深圳印象

五洲传播出版社
China Intercontinental Press

A Tapestry of the Old and the New
新旧画卷

湾区明珠

Culture and Arts
艺文雅韵

艺术理想

Azure Sea and Verdant Mountains

碧海青山

奇遇自然

The Timeless Charm from a Fresh Perspective

古趣新姿

老城往事

A Tapestry of the Old and the New

新旧画卷 湾区明珠

Chung Ying Street

A Century of Stories with the Sea Breeze Ever Present

中英街 | 海风吹不断的百年

As dawn's first light gently breaks, the quiet of Sha Tau Kok begins to lift, and the streets seem to come to life in an instant. This narrow, unique street has stood for over a century, connecting Hong Kong and Shenzhen. Here, people from all walks of life pass by, with shops lining the street, vibrant vintage signs hanging above, and ancient banyan trees casting their shade. The air is filled with the occasional, melodic calls of vendors speaking Cantonese, as life moves to the rhythm of the street. The elements of Chung Ying Street resemble scenes from an old film, rich with the city's memories, with the boundary stone at the street's center serving as both a historical marker and a resilient witness to the shared triumphs and adversities of both the city and the nation. On June 9, 1898, during the 24th year of Emperor Guangxu's reign, Li Hongzhang and the British Minister to China signed the *Convention Between the United Kingdom and China, Respecting an Extension of Hong Kong Territory* in Beijing, leasing the Kowloon Peninsula and its surrounding waters to Britain for 99 years. The boundary stone, inscribed with "24th Year of Emperor Guangxu's Reign, Chinese–British Boundary Marker No. ×," divided Sha Tau Kok in two. Today, amid the tides of a new era, Chung Ying Street remains steadfast, holding onto a century of trials and tribulations, whispering tales of the past to every visitor in the sea breeze of Mirs Bay.

晨曦微露，沙头角的宁静缓缓褪去，街道仿佛刹那间苏醒，喧嚣四起。这条独一无二的狭窄街道，已经在香港和深圳两城的缝隙间历经了一个多世纪。琳琅满目的店铺、五颜六色的复古招牌、枝叶婆娑的老榕树，各地人群熙来攘往，其间偶闻粤语韵味十足的叫卖声……中英街上的元素是一帧帧满载了城市记忆的老电影。矗立在街心的界碑，既是历史的警钟，也是这座城市与国家荣辱与共、兴衰相随的坚韧见证。清光绪二十四年（1898 年）6 月 9 日，李鸿章与英国驻华公使在北京签订中英《展拓香港界址专条》，将九龙半岛及其附近海域租给英国九十九年，并以刻有“光绪帝二十四年中英地界第 × 号”的界碑，将沙头角一分为二。今天的中英街，在新时代的洪流中，以不变的姿态深情守护着一个世纪的风雨沧桑，于大鹏湾的海风中，为每位访客低语着往昔的故事。

Window of the World

A Night Sky Illuminated by Dazzling Fireworks

世界之窗 | 夜空之下烟花绚烂

Three decades ago, the Window of the World opened on Shennan Avenue, on Shennan Avenue as an imaginative miniature scenic area for travelers at heart to experience global wonders—from ancient marvels to modern spectacles—and revel in a variety of performances, all in just one day. On festive occasions, as night falls and the city lights begin to twinkle, fireworks bloom beneath the Arc de Triomphe like shooting stars streaking across the sky or radiant flowers shimmering, piercing the dark night. Lovers embrace tightly beneath the glowing display, travelers quietly send prayers to loved ones far away, while others simply immerse themselves in the shared joy of the moment, united in spirit despite the distance. This is the timeless allure of Window of the World—ever-changing yet constant—mirroring the spirit of Shenzhen, a city known for its bold innovation and limitless inclusivity.

三十年前，世界之窗以缩微景区这一别出心裁的方式出现在深南大道之上，使得当时憧憬远行他乡的人可以在一天之内遍览古今名胜，尽享各地歌舞。每逢佳节，夜幕降临，华灯初上，凯旋门下烟花绽放，犹如万千流星划破夜空，又似荧光花朵熠熠生辉，刺破黑暗的夜幕。有情人在烟花下紧紧相拥，游子为远方的亲人默默祈福，而更多的人则带着天涯共此时的美好祝愿沉浸其中。这是世界之窗在不停改变中不变的魅力，恰似深圳这座城市的精神风貌——勇于探索，无限包容。

Overseas Chinese Town

A Stroll Through the Enchanted Forest

华侨城 | 绿野仙踪中的穿行

Sunlight filters through the dense forest, casting a golden glow on the lush greenery of Tea Stream Valley. At the Interlaken Town train station, passengers board a vintage steam train, and as the whistle blows and the wheels start to clatter, a journey reminiscent of a Hayao Miyazaki manga gently unfolds. This forest train, among the most popular attractions in Yantian OCT, spans 5,200 meters and shuttles between Tea Stream Valley and the Grand Canyon of Chinese Town. The entire journey takes approximately 50 minutes, immersing passengers in a blend of exotic landscapes and fairy-tale scenes, creating unforgettable moments along the way.

阳光透过密林，给茶溪谷的花草树木镀上金灿灿的光辉，在茵特拉根小镇的火车站踏上复古小火车，伴随着汽笛声、铁轨的叮当声，一段仿若穿梭在宫崎骏漫画中的奇妙旅行徐徐开启。森林小火车是盐田华侨城众多项目中最受欢迎的一个，全长 5200 米，往返于茶溪谷与大峡谷之间，整个旅程约需 50 分钟。乘客们时而感觉身处异域风情，时而又如同误入一处童话秘境之中，每一瞬间都令人难以忘怀。

OH Bay

Strolls and Celebrations Above the Skyline

欢乐港湾 | 高空中的漫步与派对

The Ferris wheel at OH Bay, lauded as "The Bay Glory," stands as the tallest of its kind gracing the skies of Shenzhen. It is designed for dreamers and those who embrace life, offering a romantic "space odyssey" experience. Standing at 128 meters, its unique, large, fin-shaped structure ranks it among the world's top four panoramic Ferris wheels with large cabins. Each gentle rotation takes 28 minutes, with space capsule-like cabins lifting passengers to breathtaking heights, giving them a bird's-eye view of the bay area's enchanting vista, featuring nearby towering skyscrapers, winding interchanges, distant white sandy beaches, and the calm, azure sea.

欢乐港湾内的摩天轮被誉为"湾区之光"，是深圳上空最高的摩天轮，专为热爱幻想、拥抱生活的人提供最浪漫的"太空奇遇"。摩天轮总高 128 米，采用了世界首创的鱼鳍状异形大立架，位列世界四大全天景回转式大轿厢摩天轮之一。它以每 28 分钟一圈的速度缓缓旋转，太空胶囊般的轿厢将乘客带入高空，让他们尽情俯瞰迷人的湾区风景：近处的高楼大厦、盘旋如带的立交桥、远处如白练飞舞的沙滩、无风无浪的蔚蓝色大海。

人人
都是
艺术家

Culture and Arts

艺文雅韵 艺术理想

Sea World Culture and Arts Center

A White Romance Where Mountains Meet the Sea

海上世界文化艺术中心｜山海邂逅的白色浪漫

Along the winding coastline of Nanshan's Wanghai Road stands a modern edifice, resembling a collection of white boxes stacked with artistic precision. This structure breaks the quiet monotony of its surroundings, offering a visual contrast to the distant verdant peaks of Hong Kong's Yuen Long and the gentle waves washing against the nearby shore. Serving as a graceful note connecting the mountains and the sea, it adds a rhythmic elegance to the landscape. Since its establishment, the Sea World Culture and Arts Center—renowned architect Fumihiko Maki's first project in China—has emerged as a key cultural landmark in the Guangdong-Hong Kong-Macao Greater Bay Area. Spanning 26,000 square meters with a total building area of over 71,000 square meters, it serves as a unique cultural hub, offering a blend of exhibitions, performances, public education, and commercial activities.

在南山望海路蜿蜒的海岸线上，一栋现代建筑犹如错落有致堆积起来的白色盒子，打破了周遭的单调与孤寂。远处香港元朗的青山在天际线上隐约可见，近处海浪轻轻拍打岸边，这座建筑宛如一首连接山海的协奏曲中，一个轻巧跳跃的音符，为这片景致增添了些韵律之美。海上世界文化艺术中心自诞生之日起，便成了粤港澳大湾区重要的文化地标。作为世界著名建筑师槙文彦先生在中国的首件作品，它占地面积达2.6万平方米，建筑面积超7.1万平方米，是一个集展览、演艺、公教、商业等多种功能于一体的独特文化载体。

Shenzhen Art Museum

The City's Soulful Expression

深圳美术馆 | 城市心灵的声音

In a city known for its bold embrace of innovation, modern art has shed its reputation as an exclusive niche to become an element integral to urban life at the Shenzhen Art Museum. Once tucked away in an idyllic location surrounded by verdant hills and clear waters, the museum now stands tall amid the edifices of Shenzhen North Station, its distinctive architectural design reflecting the creativity at its core. This expansive and inclusive museum, with a sprawling area of 66,000 square meters, features 18 distinct galleries that present a wide array of artistic expressions—ranging from installation art, interwoven scapes, and light-based art to modern sculptures, classical oil paintings, and traditional ink paintings. With soft lighting throughout, visitors are invited to slow down and fully experience the profound and soulful connection that art can inspire.

在勇于创新的现代化城市中，现代艺术已不再是曲高和寡的代名词，而是深圳美术馆内触手可及的城市生活元素。脱离了老馆青山绿水环抱的得天优势，在深圳北站高楼耸立之中，美术新馆以截然不同的建筑外观向外界传达着它充满创意的内核。美术馆规模宏大、兼容并蓄，建筑面积 6.6 万平方米，拥有 18 个艺术展厅，从装置艺术、互生景观、光影艺术、现代雕塑到古典油画、传统水墨画等一应俱全。在柔和的室内光线下，每个人都可以放慢脚步，静静感受艺术对心灵的触动。

让城市
的每扇窗户
都透着阅读
的灯光

Dafen Oil Painting Village

A Dream Painted in Brushstrokes

大芬油画村 | 一支画笔的梦想

In this unique Hakka village, located in the Buji Street and spanning a mere 0.4 square kilometers, graffiti brightens the walls, oil paintings fill the quaint roadside shops, colorful verses are etched into blue stone bricks, and sculptures are scattered throughout narrow alleys, creating a one-of-a-kind artistic landscape. Artists, their clothes often streaked with paint, occasionally brush past, adding to the vibrant scene. Here, art is undeniably woven into the fabric of daily life.

Once home to just over 300 indigenous residents whose ancestors tilled the land since the Qing dynasty (1644–1911), Dafen Village was transformed into an artists' haven in the 1980s with the arrival of its first art dealer. Today, it hosts over a thousand galleries and a permanent population of 10,000 painters and artists. Over a million oil paintings are created and sold here each year, many of which are exported globally, earning Dafen its well-deserved reputation as "China's Premier Oil Painting Village."

墙壁上的涂鸦、路边小店里的一张张油画、青石砖上镌刻的彩色诗句、小巷中形态各异的雕塑，再加上偶尔擦肩而过、身上还沾着油彩的艺术家，共同构成了这座位于布吉街道、占地仅 0.4 平方公里的客家村落中独特的风景。在这里，艺术无疑成了生活必需品一般的存在。

最初，大芬村只有 300 多名原住民，他们的祖先自清朝开始便在这里种地为生。然而，自 20 世纪 80 年代第一个画商进入大芬村后，大芬村已发展成拥有千余家画廊和 1 万名常驻画工、画师的画家村。每年，这里生产和销售的油画高达 100 多万张，其中许多作品远销海外，使大芬村成为名副其实的“中国油画第一村”。

人人
都是
艺术家

The Eye of the Bay Area

A Quiet Escape Amidst the Bustle

深圳湾区之眼 | 于喧嚣中栖息精神

In the midst of busy work, there is nothing more satisfying than indulging in the pleasures of reading. The fresh scent of ink lingers as you turn the pages, and the words, in soft, dark print, unfold before your eyes. Each story takes you on a journey—sometimes calm and serene, sometimes filled with unexpected twists and turns—each moving at its own gentle, rhythmic cadence.

The Bay Area Store of Shenzhen Book City project, known as the "Eye of the Bay Area," will provide a peaceful escape from the mundane, a place to find spiritual nourishment. It is located east of the central green axis in Bao'an District's central zone, adjacent to the Bao'an District Library and the Youth Palace, with a construction area exceeding 130,000 square meters. Its design inspiration comes from the ancient wisdom of "double jade plates," which means "round sky and square earth." When viewed from the air, it looks like a pair of deep eyes staring at Shenzhen.

In the future, the "Eye of the Bay Area" will become a walking-style all-ecological cultural park, and will gather four major diversified theme integration formats of "culture + technology," "culture + tourism," "culture + art," and "culture + creativity," bringing an ultimate cultural experience beyond traditional bookstores. Here, every page of text will become a painting, and every touch of color will tell a story so that every traveler who steps into this cultural holy land can feel the shock and sublimation of the soul.

在繁忙的工作之余，阅读永远是最令人愉悦的选择。翻开散发着油墨清香的书页，一行行淡黑色的文字在眼前流淌，它们或平静祥和，或波折坎坷，缓吟慢唱着别样的故事与人生。

深圳湾区书城项目——“湾区之眼”将给予每一位深圳人一个逃离平凡、追求精神滋养的避风港。坐落于宝安中心区中央绿轴的东侧，与宝安区图书馆、青少年宫交相辉映，“湾区之眼”以超过 13 万平方米的宏伟建筑面积，傲然挺立。其设计灵感源自“双玉盘”，寓意“天圆地方”的古老智慧，从空中俯瞰，更似一双深邃的眼眸，凝望着这片热土。

未来，“湾区之眼”将成为一座漫步式全生态文化公园，同时集聚“文化 + 科技”“文化 + 旅游”“文化 + 艺术”“文化 + 创意”四大多元主题融合业态，带来超越传统书城的极致文化体验。在这里，每一页文字都将成为一幅画，每一抹色彩都将讲述一个故事，让每一位踏入这片文化圣地的旅人，都能感受到心灵的震撼与升华。

Azure Sea and Verdant Mountains

碧海青山 奇遇自然

Dameisha Beach

A Gentle Breeze over a Romantic Horizon

大梅沙海滩 | 清风拂过浪漫的尽头

Early risers are often drawn to Dameisha Beach before dawn, relishing the cool breeze carrying the faint scent of coconuts. The distant mountains resemble an ink-wash painting, while the tranquil waters rest peacefully. Overhead, layers of white clouds streak the sky, touched with a delicate blush of crimson, like icing on a cake. This beach, set between the azure sea and the verdant hills of Dapeng Bay, stretches 1,800 meters and buzzes with activity on sunny days. Visitors bask in the sun, enjoy picnics, and take part in activities like beach walks, sand sliding, and sand sculpting. Water sports such as sailing, surfing, jet skiing, and yachting are also growing in popularity. For those seeking peace, a leisurely stroll along the Yantian Seaside Promenade offers the gentle sound of waves lapping against the rocks—a perfect blend of nature's beauty, both captivating and melodious.

不甘落后于晨光的人，会赶在日出前赶到大梅沙海滩，享受椰风吹拂的缕缕清凉，远山如黛、近水沉静，空中的白云层层叠叠，宛如被一抹淡淡的猩红点缀的奶油蛋糕。大梅沙这片镶嵌在大鹏湾碧海青山间的海滩全长 1800 米，在晴朗的日子里总会热闹非凡。人们在沙滩上晒太阳、野餐，参与踩沙、滑沙及雕沙等陆上活动，帆船、冲浪、海上摩托、游艇等水上项目越来越受欢迎。偏爱宁静之人，则漫步于盐田海滨栈道，倾听海浪轻拍礁石的声音，感受自然奏响的完美乐章，迷人又动听。

Yangmeikeng

Discover the Enchanting Forested Valleys of the Volcanic Gorge

杨梅坑溪谷 | 探寻火山谷的溪谷幽林

As you drive through the green valley of Yangmeikeng, one side opens to the vast expanse of the sea, while the other reveals the rugged karst formations typical of the region. The green silhouette of Qiniang Mountain, lush and vibrant throughout the year, occasionally comes into view through your window, and its dense forests, distant sound of natural pools, and babbling brooks create a serene atmosphere. Hidden deep within the forest lies a little-known secret retreat—a natural pool fed by Qiniang Mountain, Shenzhen's second-highest peak. Its crystal-clear waters reveal smooth pebbles at its bed, with aquatic plants gently swaying in the current.

Though Qiniang Mountain may be petite and delicate, it bears traces of ancient volcanic eruptions, harboring fossil clusters from the Jurassic period and coastal erosion and deposition landforms dating back to the Quaternary period. After exploring the stream, you can unwind in the peaceful village of Yangmeikeng Pit at the entrance of the valley. The mid-mountain Yangmei trees, laden with bright red fruit, add a splash of color to the serene surroundings. The village's tranquil houses and fields, accompanied by the incessant chirping of birds, makes it an idyllic retreat for those seeking peace and seclusion.

驱车进入杨梅坑溪谷，道路一侧是一望无际的大海，另一侧则是杨梅坑中怪石嶙峋的喀斯特岩石，七娘山四季葱茏的清秀山影不时掠过车窗；山中林木茂密丰盈，天然潭水与溪谷内的潺潺水声由远及近，在这片浓情蜜意的绿色之中悠然前行。在杨梅坑的山林深处，藏着一片鲜为人知的幽林秘境——天然潭，它发源于深圳第二高山七娘山，保持着最原始的清澈水质，藏在水底中的鹅卵石、随流水飘动的水草真切可见。

七娘山虽小巧玲珑，却是火山岩喷发地，蕴藏着侏罗纪时期的化石群与第四纪以来的海蚀、海积地貌。溯溪归来，在山谷口的杨梅坑小村闲坐，只见半山腰的杨梅树果实累累、红艳欲滴，村中屋舍田地安然宁静，耳畔鸟雀不断争鸣，无疑是一处绝佳的隐居之地。

Xichong Beach and Observatory

Embrace the Wind, Ride the Waves, and Gaze upon the Milky Way

西 涌 海 滩 与 天 文 台 | 迎 风 踏 浪 仰 望 银 河

Perched atop the summit of Xichong Mountain, the observatory stands as a beacon for astronomy enthusiasts. As the country's first comprehensive observation system that seamlessly integrates astronomical observation, meteorological monitoring, science education, and research with both in-person and online viewing capabilities, it features a state-of-the-art astronomy center, meteorological facilities, and world-class instruments. In the evening, visitors can revel in the stunning sunset over the sea, all from the pristine natural beauty of Xichong Beach. As night falls, visitors can head to the observatory for an unforgettable rendezvous with the starry sky. In this peaceful setting, the bright Big Dipper serves as your guide on your quest to uncover the mysteries of the universe. While light pollution obscures the grandeur of the Milky Way in many cities around the world, here, you can use star charts to find rare constellations like Eridanus and Centaurus, seldom seen in the Northern Hemisphere. On clear nights, if you are lucky, you might even catch a glimpse of the awe-inspiring Milky Way—26,000 light-years away—unfolding before your very eyes.

位于西涌山巅的天文台是众多天文爱好者的心之所向。作为国内首个集天文观测、气象监测、科普教育与业务研究、现场观测与网络观测于一体的综合观测系统，它配有完整的天文楼、气象楼以及世界顶尖水平的观测设施。傍晚，游客可以在保留着自然与原始韵味的海滩上欣赏颜色绚丽旖旎的海上夕阳；夜幕降临，则可移步天文台，去兑现心中那份与星空的约定。此时，夜空中最耀眼的北斗七星灿然夺目，引领着你探寻星空的奥秘。据统计，全球有许多城市因光污染已难以目睹银河的壮丽，而在这里，循着星图，你还能发现北半球难得一见的波江座、半人马座……若逢晴朗天气，幸运的话，仅凭肉眼，便能目睹到距离我们 2.6 万光年的壮丽银河。

Fairy Lake Botanical Garden

Embrace the Essence of Life in a Verdant Oasis

仙湖植物园 | 在绿色王国里感知生命

Nestled in a subtropical monsoon climate zone, Fairy Lake Botanical Garden showcases a unique beauty in every season. In spring, gentle rains nourish the land, turning it into a lush green paradise. Peach blossoms and azaleas bloom in vibrant harmony, transforming the orchard into a breathtaking sea of flowers that captivates all who pass by. In summer, the trees grow dense and vibrant, while the ravine rainforest remains a cool refuge. Here, banyan trees stretch their aerial roots, while mosses and ferns flourish in this ideal environment, weaving together a rich tapestry of life. As autumn breezes sweep through, the bald cypress by the lake takes center stage, its golden leaves deepening in hue and drifting onto the water's surface, as if whispering the poetry of life. In winter, Fairy Lake is adorned in a vintage palette of tawny, deep green, and crimson. The air is filled with the enchanting fragrance of wax plum trees, while the cycad garden is adorned with branches laden with red seeds.

As you stroll leisurely through the garden, the air is alive with a continuous chorus of birdsong. Occasionally, a graceful egret glides over the lake, while a kingfisher patiently awaits its prey by the water's edge. Adding to this vibrant tableau are the resplendent fork-tailed sunbirds, crimson minivets, and scarlet-backed flowerpeckers, fluttering elegantly through the sky. These birds are more than just lively additions to the landscape; they are the enchanting spirits that live in harmony with the surrounding flora.

即便位于亚热带季风气候区，仙湖植物园仍以其四季更迭展现出截然不同的风姿。春季细雨纷纷，万物青绿，桃园中桃花与杜鹃竞相开放，花海的浪潮几乎要将漫步其中的游人淹没。夏季，树木葱葱茏茏，沟谷雨林区却显得格外清凉，大榕树长出无数气根，苔藓与蕨类在最适宜的温度下编织着生命的篇章。秋风起时，落羽杉成了湖畔的主角，金黄色的叶片渐次浓郁，铺染了整个湖面，仿佛在低语生命的诗意。而冬季则以复古的棕黄、墨绿与深红点缀仙湖，一树树蜡梅散发令人沉醉的幽香，苏铁园内红豆满枝。

园中闲走，鸟鸣不断，时而可见白鹭轻盈掠过湖面，翠鸟在湖边静待捕食，更有色彩斑斓的叉尾太阳鸟、赤红山椒鸟、朱背啄花鸟翩然起舞，这些鸟儿是活泼的风景，更是与植物共生的精灵。

The Timeless Charm from a Fresh Perspective

古趣新姿 老城往事

Dongmen Old Street of Luohu

A Tapestry of Market Life Through the Ages

罗湖东门老街｜墟市里的流光岁月

The name "Shenzhen" first appeared in historical records in 1410, during the eighth year of Emperor Yongle's reign in the Ming dynasty. In the Cantonese and Hakka dialects, "Zhen" refers to a ditch or water channel between fields. The village was named "Shenzhen" because of its abundant water bodies and a deep channel running through the fields.

Nestled between Hong Kong and Guangzhou, this area has thrived as a bustling market hub owing to its strategic location, evolving through the tides of history into a renowned commercial center. Dating back 300 years, this was the lively east gate ("east gate" pronounced "dongmen" in Chinese) of Shenzhen Market, where blue-bricked Cantonese arcades stood alongside Lingnan-style buildings in a charming, picturesque disarray. For those seeking the soul of the city, Siyue Academy within Dongmen Old Street is a must-visit. Once a cultural haven for the residents of Shenzhen Market, it served as a repository of knowledge and a vessel of memories spanning centuries. The east gate of the market, much like a cultural and spiritual totem, has been cherished by generations. Though today's Dongmen Old Street is a bustling pedestrian thoroughfare, lined with modern shopping malls and thronged with visitors, the essence of this place remains untouched by the passage of time and the many transformations it has witnessed over the years.

"深圳"之名，始见于明永乐八年(1410年)的史籍之中。"圳"在广府白话和客家方言里意指田间水沟。因村中水泽遍布，且有一条深水沟穿田而过，故得名"深圳"。

地处香港与广州之间，因位置得天独厚，这里逐渐兴起墟集，在历史的变迁之中成为远近闻名的商贸中心。回溯300年前，这里是繁华的深圳墟市东门，彼时，青砖黛瓦的广府骑楼和岭南建筑错落有致，交相辉映。对追寻城市灵魂的人来说，东门老街内的思月书院是个值得探访的地方，它曾是"深圳墟"居民汲取文化知识的精神粮仓，承载着数百年的点滴记忆。墟市的东门，如同一种文化和精神的图腾被传承了下来，尽管如今的东门老街已是一条拥挤着一座座现代化购物商场、游人如织的步行街，但匆匆光阴之下，经年累月的变迁似乎并未改变其本质。

Dapeng Fortress

Six Centuries of Turbulent History

大鹏所城 | 烽烟沉浮六百年

“Among coastal fortresses, Dapeng stands supreme.” Established in 1394, during the 27th years of Emperor Hongwu’s reign in the Ming dynasty, and officially named the Dapeng Garrison Thousand-Household Fortress, Dapeng Fortress served as a vital maritime defense stronghold during both the Ming and Qing dynasties. It is renowned for its ability to repel invasions despite being outnumbered, earning widespread acclaim for successfully resisting British forces. Throughout its distinguished six-century history, the fortress produced many commanders and generals, immortalized in historical records, earning it the prestigious title of “Village of Generals.”

Strolling through the ancient city’s old alleys, the air feels humid, and the gentle sunlight casts a warm glow over the smooth, reflective cobblestone streets. Lush banana trees and clumping bamboo thrive in front of the old courtyards, while gentle wisps of smoke rise from the eaves, blending with the hum of motorcycles winding through the narrow lanes. As you explore the well-preserved generals’ residences, with their deep courtyards, you can almost catch a glimpse of the splendor of lives once lived amidst the tumult of battle. It serves as a touching tribute to the past and a cherished remembrance for those who hold onto these relics of history.

“沿海所城，大鹏为最”，大鹏所城本是明清时期至关重要的海防军事要塞，始建于明洪武二十七年（1394年），全称为“大鹏守御千户所城”。它曾以寡敌众，多次抵御和抗击外敌入侵，并因成功抗击英军而名扬四海。在长达六百年的辉煌战绩中，这里涌现了十几位被载入史册的将帅，他们为大鹏所城赢得了“将军村”的荣誉。

漫步在古城的老巷中，空气温润，阳光和煦，石板路光滑鉴人，老院前的芭蕉树、凤尾竹生长旺盛，屋檐之上冉冉的炊烟附和着狭窄街巷里穿梭而过的摩托车声，探寻那些保存完好的将军府邸，庭院深深，仿佛能窥见故人戎马一生的辉煌，也是今人留守旧物的纪念与怀恋。

Nantou Ancient Town

Where Time Cannot Diminish the Splendor

南头古城 | 时光散不尽繁华

The ancient archway of Nantou Ancient Town, with its elegantly upturned eaves, stands in striking contrast to busy traffic of Shennan Avenue. Beyond the archway, the majestic ancient city gate rises, silent yet steeped in profound history. The weathered, timeworn bricks of the city walls seem to whisper stories of tales of bygone eras. Meanwhile, the plaque above the gate, with bold black characters on a white background, proudly proclaims "Lingnan's Strategic Town," reminding every visitor of this city's 1,700-year journey through the storms of time. Passing through the dim gateway feels like crossing the boundaries of time, where the old and the new sharply contrast. The Xinguo Marquis Wen Family Ancestral Hall, Dongguan Chamber, South City Gate, and Baode Ancestral Hall are not merely relics of the past but also enduring testaments to the ancient city's original layout. From the establishment of Dongguan County in 331, during the sixth year of Emperor Cheng's reign in the Eastern Jin dynasty, to its renaming as Xin'an Ancient Town in 1573, the first year of Emperor Wanli's reign in the Ming dynasty, and its later transformation into Xin'an County and Bao'an County during the Republican era, this place has always been the heart of the city.

In 1953, the Bao'an County government relocated from Nantou to Shenzhen Town. Looking back, Nantou is undoubtedly the birthplace of Shenzhen, where the city's history began and evolved over centuries. Today, amidst the ancient blue bricks and tiles, the old town is alive with a myriad of new shops, each vying for attention. These establishments, whether preserving tradition or introducing innovation, offer sumptuous delicacies and traditional crafts, carrying forward the rich legacy of Lingnan and Cantonese culture that has thrived for centuries.

南头古城飞檐翘角的古牌坊与深南大道的车水马龙形成了鲜明的对比。牌坊之后，矗立着雄伟的古城门，它静默无言，却承载着厚重的历史。城墙之上，一块块陈年砖石斑驳陆离，仿佛在诉说往昔的风霜岁月。城头白底黑字的匾额上，“岭南重镇”四字赫然在目，提醒每一位到访者，这是一座历经 1700 多年风雨沧桑的古城。穿过昏暗的门洞，仿若穿越了时空，簇新与旧意被彻底分隔。信国公文氏祠、东莞会馆、南城门洞、报德祠等广府古建，不仅是历史的遗珠，更是古城格局的见证。自东晋咸和六年（331 年）设东官郡始，经明万历元年改名新安故城，再到民国时期的新安县、宝安县，无论哪个朝代，这里一直都是城市的核心。

1953 年，宝安县政府从南头迁往深圳镇，追根溯源，南头无疑是深圳的源头，是城市脉搏的起点，其历史积淀并非一朝一夕所能形成。在青砖古瓦的时光中，今日的古城内，无数新店铺竞相林立，它们或复古或创新，或提供饕餮美味或展示传统工艺，承袭了岭南广府千百年来的繁华。

Gankeng Hakka Town

A Hidden Spiritual Haven

甘坑古镇｜角落里的精神家园

Nestled beneath the busy Xiufeng Interchange, the peaceful Gankeng lies quietly among verdant hills, just a stone's throw from the highway. Bathed in sunlight, the ancient bluestone paved roads are lined with traditional Hakka walled houses, their dark-tiled roofs and whitewashed walls exuding timeless charm. A cheerful stream winds gracefully between the neatly arranged row houses, adding to the serene beauty of this hidden gem.

For 350 years, Gankeng Town has stood since the Hakka people migrated south from the Central Plains and settled in Shenzhen. With their characteristic ingenuity and craftsmanship, the Hakka transformed this once mountainous wilderness into a village where buildings appear to grow within buildings, evoking scenes of paintings within paintings. The watchtowers, Diaolou, and stilt houses are arranged with artistic grace, connected by winding alleys that guide each household to serene vistas. Historical landmarks such as Zhuangyuan Tower, Nanxiang Tower, and Guandi Temple also reflect Gankeng's rich historical legacy. Meanwhile, the Anhui-style architecture of Shouzi Tower, Feng Tower, Fuzi Tower, and Qilin Tower, with their intricately carved beams and painted rafters, exudes a distinctive cultural charm. Traditional arts like shadow puppetry, the *qilin* dance, and the Hakka hat (also known as the "Lord Su's hat") continue to thrive, passed down through generations of Gankeng residents. Gankeng not only steadfastly preserves the essence of Hakka culture but also serves as a hidden spiritual haven within the modern city, evoking nostalgia, warmth, and healing.

在繁忙的秀峰立交桥下，甘坑悄然隐匿于距离高速路咫尺之遥的绿色山峦之中。阳光下，古旧的青石板路两旁，一幢幢客家围屋以黛瓦白墙展露古朴之美，欢快的溪流在错落有致的排屋间潺潺流淌。

自中原南迁的客家人定居深圳以来，甘坑已历经350年的沧桑岁月。他们凭借客家人的智慧与巧手，将这块山间荒野打造成了楼中有楼、画中有画的村落。炮楼、碉楼、吊脚楼错落有致，家家户户房巷相连相通，每一条小路都曲折蜿蜒，通向幽深的景致。状元楼、南香楼、关帝庙等古迹，承载着甘坑厚重的历史记忆；而寿字楼、凤楼、福字楼、麒麟楼等徽派建筑，则以雕梁画栋、精雕细刻的技艺，彰显着独特的文化韵味；皮影戏、舞麒麟、客家凉帽（亦称“苏公笠”）等传统艺术，也在甘坑人的传承下大放异彩。甘坑，不仅坚定地守护着客家文化的精髓，也是隐于现代化城市中的精神家园，多情、怀旧、温暖且治愈。

图书在版编目（CIP）数据
深圳印象 : 汉英对照 / 陈曦著. -- 北京 : 五洲传播出版社, 2025. 1. --（中国城市）. -- ISBN 978-7-5085-5298-9
Ⅰ. K926.53
中国国家版本馆CIP数据核字第20246LB448号

中国城市：深圳印象
Chinese Cities：Shenzhen Impressions

出 版 人：关　宏
责任编辑：杨　雪
助理编辑：汪梦琦
插　　画：玖玥工作室　王建华
文　　字：陈　曦
译　　者：潘英赵
审　　校：Lee Shee Yik
设计策划：山谷有魚
装　　帧：张伯阳
出版发行：五洲传播出版社
地　　址：北京市海淀区北三环中路 31 号生产力大楼 B 座 6 层
邮　　编：100088
发行电话：010-82005927，010-82007837
网　　址：http://www.cicc.org.cn，http://www.thatsbooks.com
印　　刷：北京市房山腾龙印刷厂
版　　次：2025 年 1 月第 1 版第 1 次
I S B N：978-7-5085-5298-9
开　　本：889mm × 1194mm　1/32
印　　张：6
字　　数：20 千
定　　价：49.8 元